Aunt Bea

Aunt Bea

The Treasured Memories of My Jewish Mother

Jerry E. Feldman

Writers Club Press

San Jose New York Lincoln Shanghai

Aunt Bea
The Treasured Memories of My Jewish Mother

Writers Club Press
an imprint of iUniverse.com, Inc.

For information address:
iUniverse.com, Inc.
620 North 48th Street, Suite 201
Lincoln, NE 68504-3467
www.iuniverse.com

ISBN: 0-595-13941-8

Printed in the United States of America

CONTENTS

CHAPTER ONE

"Have you told mother that you're divorced yet?" intoned my oldest sister Joyce from the other end of the phone. I had been divorced from my wife of 26 years for 2 months without telling my 84 year old mother and somehow this bothered my sister.

When I answered "no," she sternly, in older sisterly tones told me off, ending with, "Well, damn it, call her today and tell her or I will."

I obediently told her I would and took the bull by the horns, stopped everything I was doing in the office and called mother. We made a date to meet the next day for some pie and coffee at Mammies, her favorite restaurant, located on Randolph street across from Marshall Fields in Chicago's loop. Six days a week, in mid afternoon, mother stopped in for a bite, but more importantly, she stopped for the conversation.

I spent that night alone in my bed, tossing and turning, trying out different scenarios in my mind for breaking the news to mom. It would hit her like a lighting bolt as she could not possibly have expected my wife and me to break up. We seemed to be an ideal suburban family with four boys, three of them already adults, two married and a settled place in our suburban community that reeked of happiness.

The next afternoon, upon entering Mammies, I spotted mom seated at the counter sipping coffee while chatting amiably with her waitress and climbed up on a stool next to her.

"Hi sweetheart", I said as I gave her a kiss on her delicious, soft, apple shaped cheek that had the skin of a twenty year old. Her face lit up with a huge smile as it always did when we met as she kissed me back fourfold. I sipped some coffee while she finished her daily apple pie a la mode along with her coffee and listened to the waitress tell me what a wonderful mother I had.

After mom and I had chatted for a few minutes about her grandchildren and my successes, I haltingly said,

"Mom, there's something I have to tell you."

She looked kindly at me with questioning eyes,

"What is it darling?"

"Marilyn and I got divorced," I quickly blurted out and stopped awaiting her reaction as I couldn't think of what to add. There was a momentary pause as she looked at me with her loving eyes and finally said philosophically,

"Darling, everything happens for the best."

After a short pause, she quickly followed with,

"And I never liked her anyway."

I could only grin and hold her tightly, this wonderful mother of mine.

No matter what went wrong in my life, from the earliest recollection of childhood on, mother, Bea, Becky, grandma Bea, dearie or Aunt Bea as she was fondly called by friends and relatives, never once wavered in her sweet love and affection for me. She remained, till her death 20 years ago, that one in a million person who loved the world and everyone in it, one who always saw the good in everybody and possessed a true spirit of life until the end.

She wasn't interested in why, how come, or what happened to my marriage of twenty six years. She didn't really mean having not liked her, of course she did. She only wanted to show me where her heart was and whose side she was on. She didn't try to affix blame on either party. She didn't tell me we should have had counseling or seen a Rabbi. She never said, "What will people say?" She didn't question what our children said. She didn't whine about what her friends would say. Only one thing dominated her thoughts that moment, her son, his well being and his happiness.

If she were to have just been told I was a fiend like the Boston Strangler, Speck or Manson, it wouldn't have mattered to her. Oh she might have said something like "Did you have to kill so many darling" but that would have been as far as she would have gone.

For years I've regaled my friends with stories about Bea and they keep coming back asking for repeats or new ones. Pals of mine that grew up with me all have an Aunt Bea story or two and everyone else that knew her could also come up with their share. She was such a gem, such a rare individual such a loving person, that I knew someday I would have to spread the word about Aunt Bea to others. I would have to give this lady to the world for the years to come so that just maybe, one or more persons would become an Aunt Bea because of it. So I took my word processor in hand and began her story.

CHAPTER TWO

My relationship with Bea, my mother, was spelled L-O-V-E. Whenever I think of her, love enters and permeates my vision. When I dream of her a feeling of warmth and happiness takes hold of my soul. From the earliest moments of my childhood memory and throughout my adult life I was called dear, darling, sweetheart, Jerry dear, sunshine, golden hands, or sonny. I never heard stinker, brat, bad, rotten or words of that ilk.

I was always made to feel that I was the apple of her eye and could do no wrong in her mind. I was never spanked or slapped by her nor was I ever humiliated in the presence of others. I was never disciplined or punished nor did she ever holler or scream at me. I was never sent to my room, denied a meal or dessert or had my radio or phonograph player taken from me. When the time came, in my teens, to begin going out with the guys and dolls, she never once told me to be in at a certain time. I grew up trusted completely by her and I responded to that trust by seldom giving her cause for worry.

There were times of course that I slipped, didn't call or write as I should have, stole money from her purse, or was fresh, but she never criticized me because of them. I can only remember her with a smile on her face. Oh sure, there were times when sadness enveloped her for various reasons and the smile disappeared for a short while but those times were few and far between.

She was truly loved by everyone she touched, her family, her friends, my friends and friends of my sisters as well as everyday persons she ran across. Just the other day while I was writing a chapter of this book, an old friend of my sister's called. When I told her about some diary entries that mother left behind which concerned her mother, she insisted I bring them along when we were to meet in Tucson later in the month. She couldn't wait to read some stories of mother and talk about her with me.

CHAPTER THREE

I lost my 51 year old dad, Barney, when I was only seven years old, to a sudden, swift and fatal heart attack that occurred during a party mother and he were hosting at our house on Farwell Avenue in Chicago on October 21, 1933. They had a huge amount of friends whom they loved to entertain and this Saturday night affair was no different from any other fun filled party they threw. But by ten o'clock on that cool, breezy October evening, dad wasn't feeling quite right and asked his dear friend Jack Cohn to take a walk with him so he could get some fresh air.

The two of them left the festive party and walked casually toward Lake Michigan beach front. But shortly thereafter only one returned to excitedly shout for someone to call the fire department which quickly arrived and tried in vain to resuscitate my dad who lay still on the sidewalk near the house.

I was awakened shortly thereafter by my older sisters, Joyce and Blossom, who told me something terrible had happened to daddy, but at the age of seven I couldn't quite comprehend what that meant. I just sat up in bed trying to hear what the muffled voices outside my bedroom were saying as I clutched my big stuffed dog Pal out of fear.

What I did hear loud and clear that evening was a terrible wailing sound that I couldn't readily identify. But the next morning while I lay in the parlor on my stomach reading the Sunday comics, I heard it again, this time coming from my mother's bedroom and I realized it was mom. When I entered her room I found her crying inconsolably and I finally began to realize that daddy wasn't around to comfort her and that he might never be around again.

Up until that time I could only remember wonderful soft, sweet, kind things happening around our house, forgetting of course the mean nasty things that my two sisters did to their kid brother. But mom and dad were always there to shield me from those two fiends. They were always there to let me into their bed when I was frightened by a particularly bad dream or when Joyce or Blossom would scare me half to death with monster stories.

They were especially there the night after mom and dad took me to see the movie *King Kong.* No way was I going to sleep alone in my bed with only my big stuffed dog Pal to protect me against that big hairy monster with the drooling fangs. I needed the warmth and feel of my dad and mom and so I hopped out of my bed and into theirs, quick like a fox, and squnched myself in between them pulling the covers over my head.

But even when I finally got comfortably nestled under the covers, I just had to open my eyes and peek towards the second floor window of their room out into the moonlit night. Damned if King Kong's head wasn't staring back at me with those huge, fierce eyes and gigantic fangs dripping with blood. Yeow, my head went right back under the covers and I never saw anything more until the morning's light when mom woke me for kindergarten class with a hug and a kiss.

Dad's funeral was held at our nearby Temple and my closest buddy Donald Dooley came along to sit with me wearing a yarmulke (skull cap) for the first time. I don't recall anything about the crowd or the service as my conscious mind has obviously blocked the scene out completely. In fact, I hadn't even remembered my friend Donald being there until he and I got together recently on the telephone for the first time in 60 years and I listened while he painted a word picture of the two of us sitting side by side during the service.

The service was followed by a long drive out to the Waldheim Cemetery in suburban Forest Park that ended as I watched my father's coffin entering a large freshly dug excavation. All the while, I could hear mother's sobs and moans amidst her plaintiff pleadings of "Barney, Barney, how could you leave me?"

For there she was, a 43 year old widow with three children aged 7, 9 and 12. There was another daughter, Thelma, who would have been fourteen but who had died eight years earlier from peritonitis after her appendix burst when she was six. Mother often told me the story of how Thelma had had a stomach ache for a number of days which she believed was caused when she swallowed a penny, and none of the home remedies seemed to help. Remember, this was 1922 and I don't think we had specialists in pediatrics in those days nor did we know what reaction a penny had on ones stomach.

Nevertheless, mother finally called the doctor who listened to her describe Thelma's symptoms and promptly told her to give Thelma some castor oil. Mother followed the doctor's advise and gave Thelma a big dose of that stuff and she promptly got worse and the pain became excruciating. When mother finally decided that Thelma had more than a mere stomach ache, she and dad took her to the hospital where it was discovered that her little appendix had burst and its poisons were spreading throughout her abdomen. Without today's antibiotics, nothing could have saved her and mother experienced her first tragedy.

I'm sure that these two events, the deaths of dad and Thelma were more than instrumental in forging mother's character for the next 46 years of her life, for she always used the expressions "everything happens for the best" or "it's bashert" (it's fate) and believed deeply in them. I'll never know whether or not these expressions developed during her up-bringing in a Jewish home. God knows she and her parents, both of whom had come from Russia and its pogroms had to have faith in Him just to keep going at times. Nor will I ever know whether or not my dad instilled it in her during their seventeen year marriage. Nevertheless, her deep belief in fate forged her character and outlook on life.

What I did know was that it was a beautiful and comforting belief that seemed to sustain her through all future hardships.

CHAPTER FOUR

There I was, all of seven years old, when mom put her arms around me a few days after dad's funeral and said to me with oh so sad eyes,

"Now sweetheart, you're the man of the house."

Wow, was I ever floored. Seven years old and I was chosen to be the head of a household that included those two monster sisters, mom, our maid Edna and Brownie our terrier. Wow.

The duties of the "man of the house" began when mother and her father, Grandpa Mendell sat me down and told me that since I was the only son, I would have to say Kaddish (prayers) for my dead father each morning at sunrise and each evening at sunset for the next year. There was no arguing or ranting about the instructions as they came from mother and grandpa and you didn't question either. In those days children grew up paying close attention to the discipline of the house and rarely questioned it except to their friends. When I would be with my childhood friends Milt and Ted we would often discuss how our mothers would "hak us a chainik" (yak, yak, yak) but would not dare to tell them to their faces. It was a much finer era of family life than what I see around me today.

The next morning grandpa picked me up around 6:30 AM and took me to the temple where he sat me down and had me listen to the service. All I saw were old, old, men, many with beards and wearing hats indoors, all chanting away in some foreign language and boy did some of them have bad breath. The service lasted about 30 minutes and I was then free for the day until grandpa again picked me up, this time around 5:00 PM, to repeat the morning ritual.

From then on, morning and night, at sunrise and sundown, I trudged to the Temple before school, even before reading the comics, and quit the afternoon baseball or football game early in order to perform my duties. I walked alone down Morse Avenue in 10 degree below weather while watching the sun fight its way into the sky from behind dark depressing clouds, I hiked through mounds of snow, and got soaked in rainstorms, got up late and raced to temple, left my pals in the middle of a ball game and nothing stopped me for 365 days.

I don't recall grumbling much to myself or anyone else for that matter because I didn't seem to have any choice since mom and grandpa told me to do it. It had to be done. I had no idea what the Hebrew words meant but due to mother's encouraging words about how proud she was of her big boy, I continued to observe my people's ritual of saying Kaddish for a deceased father for one full year.

The only consolation I had from shlepping (dragging) my body to and from the Temple during the next year was when mother would give me five dollars, about once a month, to put into the Karen Ami (charity box). The five bucks never made it totally into the box because the candy store would drag me like a magnet into its wondrous surroundings and I would always spend a couple of dollars on penny candy for myself and friends and put the balance in the box. You can't imagine how much penny candy I got for two dollars, a huge super-market sized bag full. I had learned to be a gonif (a thief) early in life.

CHAPTER FIVE

Some six months after my dad died, mother met Sidney Neiman, a bachelor, and from that day on, until her death 45 years later, she and Sid were a twosome.

Sid walked over to our apartment on Lake Shore Drive every night since he lived only three blocks away. He was a nice looking man about five foot ten, a few years younger than mom, rather portly, with a head of black hair, a dapper mustache, and loved his cigars. He was completely non athletic but kept up on the happenings of the Cubs and Bears which made me like him. He dressed well at all times and I can never remember him in anything except a dress shirt, tie and a nicely pressed suit. He was a graduate attorney who never practiced the law, opting instead to go into real estate sales, a field in which he never attained any great success.

He saw mother just about every night of the week and more often than not they would go out to a late ten o'clock double feature movie followed by a bite to eat at one of the local restaurants, then back to the house when he would leave around two every morning.

He was a good companion for her but as kids we weren't especially won over to him because he appeared to be a mooch in our eyes as we saw how mother seemed to be paying for most everything they did. We were still too young and too self-ish in our thinking to understand that it was her life to lead and how we felt meant little so long as he never abused us or her in any way. He was always pleasant, and liked to talk about the many big deals that others were making around town and how he always just missed out.

But to us, he was an intruder. We kids were self centered. We wanted mother just for us, never ever stopping to realize how lonely she would have been without him as her daily companion. But that didn't matter to us. We wished that Sid would go elsewhere.

With him, mother always had company and never had to spend a day alone after all of us left home and got married and moved into homes of our own. The two of them had a lovely social life with lots of friends and did all the things that married couples have done for ages, have dinner parties, go to restaurants, play cards, go to social and entertainment events, argue, fight, make up, love and enjoy the good life.

During the next twenty or so years their relationship continued to grow and we never heard a word about marriage. They always seemed to be comfortable with one another and rarely did we kids ever hear them in an argument and never did we hear them utter bitter words about each other in front of us. They just seemed to be the ordinary middle aged couple that makes up the bulk of everyday life in this country. Neither of them had any reason to get up early in the morning so their evenings never started until he came over, about 8PM.

To us kids, mother always referred to him as Mr.Neiman
and so it remained for many years until we all ripened, had
kids of our own, and started to call him Sid. But even then,
when mother spoke of him, from force of habit, she referred
to him as Mr.Neiman. For many years we still didn't warm up
to Sid even though he never gave us any reason to dislike him.
Finally, in 1954 when mother and Sid were in Miami Beach
visiting my sister Joyce who had recently moved there, Joyce
made the decision that after 20 years of going steady, even
with her children's resentments, they ought to be married.
And so they were. I received the wedding announcement call
back in Chicago and felt happy for the two of them, especially
Sidney. Now the guy wouldn't have to walk home alone every
night in the wee hours of the morning. What a difference
forty years makes. If he tried that today he'd be mugged
before he got one block away.

CHAPTER SIX

Bea was born in Chicago in 1889, the daughter of Russian immigrant parents who came to this country around 1875. Her father Mendell was a tinsmith but I never knew him to work at anything. He was just grandpa to me. Grandma Sonya was old world through and through and spent her time at home raising five children and taking care of the home.

Mother was born Rebecca but when she got to school she found that there were five other Rebeccas around so she did the pragmatic thing and changed her name to Beatrice. Whether or not this was a legal change with all the formalities attended to it or not I don't know. She was Bea to everyone but her three older brothers Joe, Max and Paul who continued to call her Becky throughout their lives. She had a younger sister Lillian, who died of cancer at 30 leaving a four year old son Tom Gordon who became mother's pet nephew and my dearest friend.

When mother was about 14 she and her friends heard that they were hiring workers at a candy factory near her house on Chicago's near west side. They all applied and got jobs as there were no child labor laws yet in this country and the company could get by with paying them a lot less than adults doing the same work. Fourteen year olds and candy had a natural affinity for each other and the girls ate all the candy they could while at work and even managed to figure out a way of having some candy follow them home.

They all wore middy blouses that had a string tie at the waist which let the tops of the blouses billow out, a natural repository for pieces of candy. Every day when they left the factory they each seemed to have gained weight since the time they came to work. The girls had it made until one afternoon, while chatting with her supervisor, mother's middy blouse string suddenly broke and at least five pounds of candy cascaded out onto the floor as she sheepishly looked down and blurted out some teen age prattle about how it got there. A quick check of the other girls' blouses revealed a cache of candy in each. That was the end of the job for all of them and for mother it was the end of her work career. I don't think she ever worked another day in her life. At least she never told me about any subsequent job.

CHAPTER SEVEN

A few months after my dad died we moved from our apartment on Farwell to a north Lake Shore Drive high rise across from Waveland Park which was on the lake. Boy was it ever exciting to take an elevator run by an operator 15 stories up and down every day, to live 5 blocks from my beloved Wrigley Field and to make so many new pals in the building, Alan, Sonny, Warren, Ralph, Monte, Dickie and Malcolm.

Bea furnished that apartment very elegantly with all the bric-a-brac, Sevres vases, Capi di Monte and Louis XIV furniture that she and my dad had accumulated during their big income days. My father had been making an excellent living during all of their married life, first as the owner of three pharmacies on Chicago's near west side and then as a partner with Uncle Joe, mother's brother, in the pawn business.

Dad had immigrated to this country from Russia in 1898 when he was 16, learned the language, worked, put himself through Northwestern University and became a licensed pharmacist. During succeeding years he brought his parents and brothers over here to save them from the pogroms against the Jews then going on in Russia. These Russian pogroms were a forerunner to Hitler's Holocaust.

Mother and dad began going together about 1911 and soon became engaged to be married. But even at that early age mother could never make up her mind one way or another, a trait she displayed throughout her life. They stayed engaged for five years until grandpa literally threatened to throw her out unless she married Barney the druggist.

During the succeeding ten years or so mother gave birth to four children and dad's business grew to three drugstores. But mother gradually became very unhappy with dad's late working hours in the drug stores and told him about it time and time again to the point he knew he better do something else. He was making and selling a lot of medicinal gin, by prescription only of course, during the days of Prohibition and it took a lot of courage to give it all up just to please his wife.

By that time, Uncle Joe had developed a very successful pawnshop downtown at Randolph and Dearborn that only dealt in diamonds, gold and watches. With a depression looming on the horizon, mother convinced uncle Joe to take dad in as a partner which he did. Dad sold his three drug stores, invested the proceeds with Uncle Joe, and from that time on had regular hours of nine to five, six days a week.

When dad died, mother was left with a considerable dividend income from the partnership along with some fairly hefty insurance money. There was no question in mother's mind that she would not have to work for the rest of her life and that she could spend freely. She became quite a sport. My sisters and I got to go to camp each summer, she met Mr. Neiman, our maid Edna became her pal, mother took Joyce and sailed for Europe on the Queen Mary, my weekly allowance became two dollars, she became known as the rich Mrs. Feldman and she found out about the racetrack.

CHAPTER EIGHT

What an experience. Mother at the race track. She sometimes took me along on Saturdays even though I was only 10. Before we could walk 10 yards from her parked car to the race track entrance, she would buy at least three tips from touts along the way. For those of you who have never heard the word, tout, before, it is a person who claims to know who the winning horse will be before the race has run and offers you that tip for a fee. If you win you are going to tell all your friends about his great talent or at least look for him again the next time you're at the track. What you don't know is that if there are eight horses in the race he gives out 8 different tips, one for each horse in the race, for the first eight buyers thus insuring that someone is going to win and make him out to be a genius.

Talk about hustlers, these guys would nail you and walk alongside of you until they convinced you that they had the winners for sure. They reminded me of the Egyptian street hawkers selling their wares amidst the ruins of old Egypt. You could buy the Info in the white envelope for two bucks, which mother promptly did, sometimes from three or four different touts.

When she got inside the track and had to decide who to bet on., She was so confused by the touts' tips, all different, she could never decide on which horse to bet. So she did the prudent thing. She bet on every horse in the race. Even at the age of 10 I knew there was something wrong with her system but couldn't get her to change. But the stories I could tell at school were great. She always had winners but by the end of the day she always lost.

Another remembrance of her is of the time while my father was still alive. She always seemed to have lots of diamonds, pearls and gold jewelry along with lots of other red, green and blue stones that looked so pretty on her neck, in her hair or on her wrist. Whenever she and dad went out she sparkled with them.

As the years passed and I became more aware of things like jewelry and their cost I asked her to show me all of her pretty things. When she did, all I saw was a bunch of costume jewelry items that didn't come close to what I remembered seeing on her when dad was alive.

When I asked her where she was hiding all the good stuff, like in a vault, she laughed and told me the story. Since my dad was in the pawn business he made loans on many beautiful items from some of Chicago's wealthiest families. Remember, he was in business from 1929 through 1933, the years of the stock market crash and ensuing great depression when men were jumping out of windows because they had lost their fortunes or owed tremendous sums of money.

Many of those who were fighters and felt the responsibility of fighting their way back, came to my father and pawned their wives' jewelry to pay off debts. So dad's safe was full of magnificent bracelets, rings, necklaces and the like. He had all sizes, shapes and colors.

Whenever he and mother were going out to a special event, she would call and ask him to bring home a specific type of jewelry and he was almost always able to oblige. When her friends saw all these valuable pieces adorning her person they all incorrectly assumed they were hers and she became known as the diamond lady. She was wise enough never to make any attempt to tell them the true story. When dad died, the borrowing stopped, but her image and reputation for having great jewelry lived on for years and years. In fact, the costume pieces that she continued to wear were thought to be the real things according to her old friends.

CHAPTER NINE

Since mother seldom had any reason to get up at any specific time in the morning, I never saw her until about ten or ten thirty when she would come out of her bedroom wearing a dressing gown. She made herself a pot of boiling water, poured it into a cup, added a tablespoonful of mineral oil (yuck) and then sat down in the kitchen sipping the scalding water as she read the morning Tribune. Guess she felt this was the way to stay regular but never in my life did I ever hear her discuss whether or not she had a problem nor did she ever complain.

It was always fun to watch when the telephone man would come to the house while she was having her hot water. Many of you might not remember that the telephone man came once a month to open up the black coin box and take out all the nickels from within. In those days, you had to deposit a nickel to complete your call or you could also use a slug, a metal disc the size of a nickel.

Well, he would lay out all the coins and slugs on the kitchen table and rapidly count and roll the nickels, always pushing the slugs to the side. The rolls of nickels would go into his black leather bag and then he would count the slugs, multiply by 5 cents and that's what mother owed the telephone company.

Bea was always a great one with people and so her best sense told her that the telephone man would probably like a drink, not water, not a coke, but booze. I never saw one who refused and she and he would sit and talk for another half hour after all the coins were rolled and she wrote a check to Illinois Bell for the slugs.

And it wasn't just the telephone man. It was the delivery man with the groceries, the cleaners, the building engineer, or whoever else would ring the back doorbell. They all had to sit and have an ounce or two with her. The most appreciative of all were the elevator men, who would leave their elevator door open, come in, sit down in the kitchen and have a drink with her. All the while they paid no attention to the incessant call signals coming from the various impatiently waiting tenants.

On top of the booze and the conversation, she always gave the person a dollar tip for the delivery. Mind you, this was in the thirties and forties and a dollar then was like a ten today. Her concept of money was that it was something to spend and others needed it more than she.

CHAPTER TEN

Eventually mother found the gambling parlor which for many years was located in Deerfield Illinois and was known as "the joint". Everyone knew it was there, the local police, the sheriff, the state police, everyone, but no one ever did anything about it until the Federal agents got into the act about 30 years later and closed it up.

Every few years, I guess enough heat was generated to the point that they were forced to move the game to a new location, first to Vernon Hills, then further north in Lake County and finally to the Illinois Wisconsin line. Each succeeding location was equipped more completely than the previous one and you could shoot craps, play roulette or blackjack but no slots.

Once mother found this place she was hooked. She went back there with her companion Sidney, maybe once or twice a week, would lose a hundred dollars or so and have a great time. In fact she was such a good customer they sent their long stretch limousine for the two of them and returned them home the same way. Having played poker with her a few times in later years, I know that she knew very little about gambling and I never could figure out what she did at the joint. Whatever it was, she had a lot of fun and loved the attention they all paid her.

One evening, an acquaintance of hers, Phil G, approached her at the joint and told her he had run out of money and the management wouldn't cash his check unless someone else endorsed it. (They probably knew full well that he was a stiff.) Mother hardly knew this fellow at all. Anyone else would have been leery about someone who was refused credit in a gambling joint, but she was so trusting it never occurred to her to doubt Phil's good intentions.

"Would you endorse this check for me Bea, I'd really appreciate it?" Phil asked.

"Of course Phil, why shouldn't I. You're such a nice man, where do I sign?" she replied, as Phil guided her hand for the $500 endorsement. He thanked her, got his money and went about his business.

Mother thought nothing more of it until a week later when she received a call from Big Don at the joint. Big Don was obviously the collector and enforcer and not the kind of person one ignored. I was standing alongside of her when the call came in and while I started sweating, the conversation proceeded something like this.

"Mrs. Feldman, do you remember the $500 check you endorsed for Phil a few nights ago?"

"Of course I do Don, isn't he the sweetest man?"

"Well Mrs. Feldman, his check bounced and so you'll have to make it good."

"Why do I have to do that?"

"Well you see Mrs. Feldman, when you endorse a check and it's no good at the bank you become responsible."

"But all I did was sign it because he asked me to. He was so nice and I'm sure he'll pay you."

"That's right Mrs.Feldman, he's very nice but his check isn't, so I have to insist that you make it good and send us your check for $500."

Now I never knew, nor did mother ever let on, if she was playing the part of dumb Dora or really was naive in this matter. Her conversation and answers to Don kept getting spacier by the minute and his frustration with it all must have grown and grown. After all, here he was, a very big man with syndicate gambling, talking to a very sweet, steady customer about making good on someone else's debt. A good five minutes later, the conversation finally ended with, "Oh, OK Mrs. Feldman, forget all about it. We'll call Phil again for the money. When are you coming out again so I can buy you a nice dinner?"" as he decided to just write the whole deal off.

CHAPTER ELEVEN

One day when I was about ten, mother took me downtown for some new pants and parked her car in the Dearborn-Lake garage just as she did every other day of the week. She drove us in her big maroon 1932 Cadillac, a four door sedan that sparkled and was noticed everywhere we went. It was summer and she had her mink coat with her. I asked why and all she would say was, "you'll see."

When we got out of the car she purposely left the coat in the back seat saying to me through the corner of her mouth, "I hope someone steals it," and then brought her index finger to her lips in the universal sign of "sshhh."

When we returned to the garage some hours later after an afternoon of shopping and noshing (eating), she went to the cashier's window to redeem her car. Once there, she was scolded by the man behind the bars for leaving her very valuable mink coat in the car where it could have been stolen except for the honesty of one of the hikers. Poor mother, not only couldn't she get her coat stolen but now she had to give the guy a five dollar reward for his thoughtfulness.

Downtown and mother were really synonymous. She went there almost every day of the week when she didn't have a luncheon or other event scheduled. After parking her car, or in later years, taking a bus or a cab, she would go to Mammie's restaurant have her pie and coffee, kibbitz with her pal the waitress and then stroll through one State Street store after another, from Marshall Field on the north end of the Loop to Morris L. Rothchild on the south and return home the way she came, around 6PM. Most of the time she wouldn't buy a thing but just being around people and chit chatting with the sales clerks and customers made every day enjoyable for her.

It was always fun to accompany her downtown as I knew that I would wind up with chocolate candy or something equally as good. One day, I met her after school and we drove downtown. After parking the car in the usual garage we made our first stop at Woolworth's on State Street near Washington where we each had a delicious hot dog with all the trimmings and chocolate sodas which were followed by a big bag of broken chunks of Hershey chocolates.

We then walked south on State street hand in hand devouring our candy until we arrived at the La Salle Street railroad station which was few blocks west of State street on Van Buren Street. Once in the station which seemed so huge and magnificent to me at that age as it bustled with passengers and became alive with the intoning of train announcements over the loud speaker amid the babble of the scurrying passengers, mother searched for a train that would be leaving within the next hour. There were all sorts of destinations listed on the 20 or so tracks and each seemed to be a far off dream for me at that age. Having found one she wanted, we walked along the platform passing the coaches and Pullmans until we came to the club car where we boarded the empty car.

As we climbed aboard, she said it would be fun to pretend we were really going somewhere. I excitedly agreed imagining how wonderful it would be to hear the conductor shout "All aboard" and hear and feel the first screech of the wheels as they spun and groaned as the train inched forward to some far off place. Once in the club car we sat down in a couple of lounge chairs and soon a white coated waiter came by to take our order. Mother ordered me a coke and a Manhattan for herself. There we sat for at least a half hour as she made up stories about where the train was going to take us.

We fantasized a lot, talking about far off places many of which I had never heard. You can't imagine how excited and thrilled I was as mother told me of New York, Miami, San Francisco or Washington D.C. as well as Yellowstone Park and the Grand Tetons. And she made me believe that we might still be aboard when the train pulled from the station and headed for one of them. I always wondered what I would do without my pajamas and clean underwear if we did take off.

My mind reeled with excitement as the smells of the steam locomotives permeated the air and mother's soft voice described a myriad of sights that I dreamed about for years to come. I've always loved trains and I think about that day so very often. Do parents today take the time to do what she did with me? Are kids too blasé to be thrilled as I was? Just make believe, but how wonderful it was.

CHAPTER TWELVE

Another sweet remembrance of mother was our once a month drive out to the cemetery to visit dad's grave. It was taken for a number of years after dad died and then like anything else, became less and less frequent to the point of just once or twice a year. She would pile my sisters and I into the Caddie and take off on the fifteen mile trip from the north side through Chicago's west side to the Waldheim cemetery located at Des Plaines and Roosevelt Road in the suburb of Forest Park. Those were the days before expressways and the trip took at least an hour each way.

Once we arrived, mother would walk us over to dad's graveside and tell us wonderful stories about his kindness and sweetness and how much he loved us all. You could tell the depth of her sorrow in her eyes and voice. How endearing it was to watch her run her fingertips over and over his glass enclosed photo attached to the gravestone. How sweet it was as she talked to daddy telling him that the children were with her.

On one of those early trips we heard an airplane up in the sky and since it was such a great novelty we all looked towards the sound of the roaring engines in an attempt to spot it. Mother then proceeded to tell us that it was on this very spot some fifteen years earlier that she saw her first biplane and how excited she was. From that day on, mother invariably would tell the same story on every visitation, always forgetting that we had heard it so many times earlier.

Once we had paid our respects to dad's memory, we all tumbled back into the car for our trip home that would include the highlight of the week, a stop at Flukey's hot dog stand on Ogden Avenue near North Avenue. For a nickel, they served a huge kosher red hot complete with pickles, mustard, tomatoes, relish and French fries, which, along with chocolate milk was nothing short of sensational. So even though our trip was a somber one, mother always managed to lighten it up with this delectable stop.

CHAPTER THIRTEEN

I discovered the game of golf when I was 12 and played at the Park District's Waveland 9 hole golf course across the street from our Lake Shore Drive apartment as often as I could for $.25 a round. I used my father's old set of wooden shafted clubs until finally mother took me down to Spaldings on State street for a real set of Kroydon steel shafted woods and irons. I fell in love with the game and got quite good at it fast. But I also knew of no other mother who buy her son a set of REAL KROYDON CLUBS. Was I ever proud of them.

Before I knew it, she wanted to know if I would like to play at the Bon Air Country Club which was a public course 25 miles away in Wheeling, a pretty long ride before expressways were built. I excitedly said yes and a few days later she let me cut school in the afternoon and we were off to play golf. I carried my big new bag around and she carried her shoes as she walked in her hose over 18 holes. I never saw her dressed in anything but dresses, no slacks or shorts, always a dress even on the golf course.

I tried so hard that day to impress mother with my new clubs but I was terrible, dubbing shot after shot. But according to her I was already better than daddy and probably the best golfer around. I knew then for sure that I had a real great lady for a mom. Just as she assured me that I was a wonderful golfer she also convinced me that my big ears were a sign of intelligence. When I dejectedly told her that my nose was not exactly for Hollywood she assured me that a nose such as mine meant I was brave. In her eyes, there just wasn't a thing wrong with me. She never saw the bad side of anything, only what was beautiful, and if not exactly that, she would convince you that it was.

About the age of 12 , while riding in the front seat of the car with her I pestered her to let me try driving. Being the sport she was, she let me lean over in front of her to steer the car. We didn't have any Drivers Ed in those days so the only thing you could do was to get someone to teach you how to do it. Boy, was it ever exciting to be cruising down Lake Shore Drive steering that big Cadillac.

By the time I was 14, I was not only leaning over, I was also shifting the gears on the floor and using the accelerator while she worked the clutch and the brakes. We were a great team. I truly don't remember how or when I learned to do everything by myself, but that wasn't important then. Mother decided I should get a license even though I was still 14 and the law then called for fifteen.

She took me to a disabled, wheelchair bound notary public, Mr. Phillips, and lied to him about my age. I still chuckle today at my answer to his question about how many miles had I driven, when I answered with a straight face, "about a million."

I never knew how she swung that license. Who am I kidding? Of course I do. She dropped five bucks on him, and I got my license without ever having to take a driving test and a year underage with a false application. From that time on I was the most popular guy around as I was the only one who had wheels. Mother always referred to the car as Betsy and so too did my friends and me. They and I took Betsy the first and Betsy the second, a black four door 1938 Buick Roadmaster, all over the city whenever mother said it was O.K. To this day my old pals can still tell you who Betsy was I and Betsy II were.

While on the subject of driving, I'm reminded that when I asked my nephew Barney what he remembered most about Grandma Bea he didn't hesitate a second before answering, "Watching her drive while she put on her make-up." He went on to tell me how often she would be sitting at a stoplight and suddenly look in the mirror and decide she needed some additional lipstick or rouge and reach for the proper ingredient in her big purse. When the light changed she was always in the process of applying the make up and after getting honked at would let the clutch out and move ahead always looking back into the mirror as she steered with one hand and managed to shift gears and apply her lipstick with the other, no easy trick.

Barney laughed loud and long as he described the sight of his grandma steering the car from side to side as it went down Lake Shore Drive weaving back and forth. Mother always pontificated how she had never had an accident but Barney was quick to remind me that she must have caused many.

Chapter Fourteen

On Saturdays as a kid, one could always find me at the movies. Like everyone else at that age, in the thirties, it was hypnotic. Mother liked them too and quite often during the Saturday or Sunday afternoon show, while sitting with my pals, I would look up to see mother searching for me. When she found me she would sit down and watch the movie with us. I thought she had paid her way in, but no. She would go to the ticket taker and ask if he minded if she looked for her son who was late coming home. Of course they would let her in without a ticket while she searched for her errant offspring. Once she found me and sat down, I would be forced to sit and watch the movie for the second time because she wouldn't leave until she had seen the whole thing.

Bea was a regular movie buff. At least three to four times a week, Sidney would come over to the house and the two of them would catch the ten o'clock last show at one of the four local houses. Afterwards they would stop for something to eat returning home around 2:30 AM, where they would talk awhile, and then Sid would walk to his apartment three blocks away. By the time she adjusted the venetian blinds to block the morning sun, puffed up all the sofa pillows, locked all the doors, checked on her children and did whatever else she had to do, it would be about 3:30 when she climbed into bed.

Watching mother work over an insurance claims adjuster was always a thing of beauty. As I mentioned earlier she had quite a bit of expensive and breakable glassware, porcelain, and china etc. that periodically would accidentally break. Being very claim conscious she would immediately call her insurance company and register a claim which would be followed up some days later with the appearance of a claims adjuster. He would determine that, yes it was broken, yes I'll write you a check and yes I'll take the broken Sevres vase with me. The first two were OK but taking the broken treasure away from mother was another story. NO WAY was she going to part with it even if it was broken.

As you would guess, like everyone else who came into the house, she would early on make a drink for the man and sometimes a second. By the time he claimed the object, she would very sweetly object to his taking the broken item asking what would his company do with a broken vase. I never saw it fail. She invariably wound up with the check and the broken item only to have it fixed by Mr. Yamamoto in his Michigan Avenue shop for a fraction of what she received in insurance.

CHAPTER FIFTEEN

My sister Joyce who only recently passed away after 52 years of marriage to her husband Bill, became engaged to him and the two of them made plans to drive down to St.Louis to spend a few days together. In 1940 this wasn't done very often by unmarried people, and there were very few mothers who would even consider allowing their daughter to make such a trip. What would the relatives think, what would friends say, most mothers would question. Not mother. She thought it was a great idea, gave her blessing and the two of them were off in Bill's golden brown 1939 Buick convertible. Mother really was a 1940 woman inside of a 1999 spirit.

Being a dutiful daughter, Joyce called home most every night to tell mother about the fun she was having, where she went, what they did and what they bought. After a few days passed, mother called Joyce and said that since she was so close, she and Bill should drive to New Orleans because it was a fun city and they should stay at the Roosevelt Hotel near the French Quarter. By Bea, New Orleans was close to Saint Louis. Joyce and Bill thought it was a great idea so they took off for New Orleans promising to call when they arrived.

All went well. They had a great time in the French Quarter and loved the Creole cooking at Antoine's and the Court of

Two Sisters. Just about the time they were supposed to leave New Orleans for the trip back to Chicago, mother got another great idea. She called to tell them of it but the hotel desk clerk informed her that they had checked out an hour earlier. I'll never know how she pulled this off but a few hours later when Bill and Joyce pulled into a gas station somewhere in Mississippi the attendant looked first at their car, then at their Illinois license plate and gruffly said to Bill, "Are you Kogen?" to which he incredulously said "yes." "Call her mother" he snarled as he pointed to Joyce and walked away as the two of them sat with mouths agape.

Mother had called the State Police in Mississippi and conned them into believing that it was a life and death situation to find her daughter and they efficiently obliged by putting the announcement on the radio.

When Joyce obediently called, mother told her in glowing terms how wonderful Miami Beach was and since they were so close they should go there. And they did. Again, Miami Beach and New Orleans were close together in Bea's mind.

When Joyce talked to mother from Miami, believe it or not, mother told them how wonderful Havana Cuba was with all the gambling and night life and that they had to go there. This was the true Bea. Life was exciting. Life should be like a party. You should always go and have fun. This was a little much even for Joyce and Bill so they declined and drove home.

A few months later Joyce and Bill were married in a lavish wedding at the Shoreland Hotel in Chicago's Hyde Park area.

Three hundred people attended and it was really a hell of an affair. Wearing tails and sporting braces on my 14 year old teeth I took my deceased dad's place and walked my sister down the aisle and gave her away. The Herbie Mintz orchestra played until 1 AM and the last guest left about 2 AM. It was a bitter cold November evening and when we went back to the car, mother, sister Blossom, Edna, Grandpa and I, the car wouldn't start and what to do. Mother didn't hesitate one moment as she led us all back into the hotel and up the elevator straight to my sister's wedding suite. Bill opened the door in his underwear and we all trooped in. You can imagine how happy they were to see us. After we called for a tow truck, mother made herself comfortable and we talked about the wedding for two hours before help finally arrived. Bill and Joyce were obviously thrilled to see us leave.

CHAPTER SIXTEEN

Growing up with a mother like Bea always filled me with a great deal of pride, especially when my buddies were over to the house. I never felt embarrassed by her actions as today's kids are when a parent tries to show some affection or attention. What could be greater for a bunch of teenagers than to have a mother empty the refrigerator and lay all the food out on the table with the words "what else can I get you?" For a Jewish mother, this was always the high point of any day. For me, it was a great feeling to know that the gang always wanted to come to my house for the slightest of reasons.

After the snack we would say good-bye to her and ring for the elevator and she would always wait in the vestibule between apartments with us until it came. As soon as the door opened up she'd kiss every single guy or girl keeping me for last as she walked me into the elevator. As the door closed we could all see her standing there blowing kisses to everyone as the elevator began its descent. But invariably, before we got five floors down, we'd get a buzz and the elevator man would stop and reverse directions back to the 15th floor. When the door opened mother would be there saying, "I just wanted one more kiss," which I would dutifully receive and once again we'd be on our way. Never was I embarrassed because of this attention and never was I razzed by my buddies because Aunt Bea was special. Maybe if kids got that kind of loving today there wouldn't be so many of them going wrong.

Just eating lunch or dinner alone with mother in the kitchen was always a wonderful experience. She would make me a sandwich or some spaghetti or leftovers and sit close to me as I gulped everything down with loads of milk. Invariably she would tell me that I should always leave something on my plate for the birds, an old expression that I'm sure she made up. Being an obedient son I would do as instructed and leave something on my plate. As I would rise to leave the table when finished, she would grab my fork and finish off what I left always saying, "It tastes much better when it's off your plate." I good naturally said, "you're the biggest bird I've ever seen" and the two of us would have a good laugh. Of course, when I didn't feel like eating I heard the old refrain that all of our parents used in those days, "eat, eat, think of the starving Chinese."

CHAPTER SEVENTEEN

In 1938, during spring vacation, mother took my sisters and I to Miami Beach for ten days, a real big thrill for me. I had never felt warm breezes and a hot sun during winter months. Palm trees were exciting to look at and the ocean front hotels were spectacular to my 12 year mind. The glamour of the train ride to Florida plus the excitement of this paradise left fond memories with me.

We stayed at the New Yorker Hotel on Collins near 15th Street and I thought I was in pig heaven. Art deco designed hotels, swimming pools, beaches, palm trees and Wolfies restaurant serving corned beef and great big kosher pickles made it my Garden of Eden. What more could a kid ask for? When I discovered and met Man Mountain Dean, the World's champion wrestler at the hotel and actually played ping pong with him I knew it couldn't get any better.

One morning, mother took all of us, including Grandpa who was also staying in Miami Beach, on the Nikko sightseeing tour, a boat ride that cruised on the waterways of Miami Beach showing everyone the homes of the rich and famous.

God forbid we should be hungry on this one hour trip, so mother stopped beforehand and bought a huge bag full of odorous corned beef sandwiches, Kosher dill pickles and soft drinks to be devoured on the ride.

After we had cruised about a half an hour, I was hungry and asked mother if I couldn't eat one of the sandwiches she brought along and she of course quickly opened the bags and handed out sandwiches to all of us. It was probably around 11:30 AM, the time when most people start to feel hunger pangs, when the five of us started munching away on the corned beef sandwiches which were redolent with the smell of garlic. We devoured every morsel of the aromatic food while the rest of the people on the boat gave us the dirtiest looks of envy that you could ever imagine. It wasn't the most swanky thing to do but mother was never one to put on any airs. When you're hungry, you eat, period.

A few days later we all went over to grandpa's motel for lunch. By this time grandpa was living with grandma's ex nurse who had taken care of her for some years before she died. Rosie was about 30 years younger than grandpa, a little zaftig, with dyed jet black hair and certainly no raving beauty but she must have looked pretty good to grandpa who at 80, believe it or not, was still sexually active. Don't ask how I knew, I just knew.

The funny part of the incident was that I had overheard mother talking to grandpa on the phone the day before. While I couldn't understand the whole conversation I was quite aware that she was telling him to fix things up in the motel room because the kinder (children) were coming over.

Mother wanted grandpa to show us that he wasn't shacking up with Rosie just because they were sharing a room together. Thus, when we entered the large motel room which he had rented for the winter, we found two beds about ten feet apart and separating them was a large sheet hanging from a clothesline. It was a scene straight out of the movie *It Happened One Night* with Clark Gable and Claudette Colbert. No one said a word about the strange setting but Grandpa had a twinkle in his eyes that only Rosie could have put there.

In 1939 mother took all three of us plus cousin Tommy to the New York World's Fair with a side trip to Atlantic City and its famous boardwalk. What a sport she was, four teenagers for two weeks without any help from anyone. I'd never do that even if I had Anthony Hopkins along as my valet.

We all had had a great time at the Fair and in New York and when we arrived in Atlantic City we checked into the Breakers Hotel which in those days was a fairly upscale place. Being a bunch of healthy, highly spirited teenagers we frolicked and romped around the hotel rooms whacking each other with pillows and having a ball until one of the pillows broke sending feathers all over the room. Still another pillow flew out an open window falling five stories to the ground below. The noise, the feathers and the missing pillow caused the manager to nab my mother that evening as we returned from dinner and he told her in so many words to go someplace else. Well, you should have heard how indignant she got. Within a few moments I heard her say, "We're leaving this place because you're nothing but a bunch of anti-Semites. I'm going to report you to the Anti-Defamation League" she threatened as she hustled her brood into the elevator. It turned out that the Breakers Hotel was the only Kosher hotel in Atlantic City.

A year earlier, my sisters and I were in Los Angeles with mother. She loved the three day train ride getting there and so did we as we traveled through the west and stretched our legs in places like Sante Fe, Cheyenne and Albuquerque. We got to see everything in town including the tar pits, movie studios, the Brown Derby, Hollywood and Vine, the Cathay Theater and the stars hand prints and foot prints in the sidewalk. We stayed at the famous Ambassador Hotel where I was in the swimming pool every possible minute and had dinner in the elegant Coconut Grove in the evening. You can't begin to imagine how exciting this was for a twelve year old. And Bea was the one who made it all possible.

When we awoke one morning, out of the clear blue sky, mother told us we were going to Catalina Island and was I ever excited because I knew that's where my beloved Cubs took spring training, thus making the ground hallowed.

We took a cab to the waterfront in Long Beach and there before my eyes was a wondrous seaplane riding the waves as it beckoned me for my first airplane ride. I had never given a thought to flying to the island. In 1938 this was beyond the comprehension of a twelve year old.

I'll never forget that take off as the plane gained speed while its pontoons carved a wake in the water as it gracefully pulled up free from the ocean and became airborne. Nor can

I forget the sight of Catalina Island majestically sitting like a jewel in the dark blue Pacific waters as it sparkled in what seemed to be a fairyland. My Cub land.

The plane landed ever so softly and as it skimmed along the waters of the harbor I thought my mom was **The Greatest Mom In the World** for taking me so close to heaven without me even having to beg her once.

After touring the island for most of the day we came back to the center of town where my star struck 14 year old sister Blossom found out that there was some kind of dance being held that evening to which an eighteen year old had invited her. Well, we were supposed to leave for the mainland around five but Blos managed to please, please, please mother until she relented and said we would stay.

Next thing I knew, mother and Blos were shopping for a new dress for the dance while my eldest sister Joyce, who was seventeen at the time, and I, sat on the street curb mumbling that mother loves her more than us. Nevertheless, Blossom danced away a few hours while mother, Joyce and I watched. Boy were we ever pissed. But the return night flight home made up for everything as the twinkling lights of Los Angeles came into view from on high as we returned to the mainland and made a soft landing at the airport from whence we had come.

CHAPTER EIGHTEEN

Edna, our German American maid, and mother, were as close as two women could be. She had started working for mother about three years before my dad passed away and their bond grew closer and closer as the years passed. She was a very bright, pretty, industrious widow of 45 or so when she started and was a wonderful influence on all of us with her rather strict disciplinary ways. She and mother spent hours together chatting about everything under the sun. We all knew better than to cross Edna for she had mother's ear and there was no way we could win. Besides, in all truth, she was usually right. Not only that we truly loved her.

On top of all that, she was a fabulous cook who could prepare anything beautifully and specialized in desserts. What more could a teenage kid want? She set gorgeous tables for mother's dinner parties and could always be relied on for a sumptuous meal. She did all of this besides cleaning and taking care of our seven room apartment.

On the afternoon of one of mother's dinner parties, Edna experience some sort of a sad event that brought about a togetherness of counseling from mother. Mother clucked her tongue a lot, Edna shed a few tears, mother put a good shot of bourbon into Edna's hands and the two of them sipped their booze together. One drink led to another and by the time the guests arrived, Edna was not all that steady on her feet, in fact, she was smashed. Mother? She was as sober as the proverbial judge.

Nevertheless, the dinner had to go on and there were about 14 persons seated around mother's magnificently carved walnut dining table. After the soup and salads had been consumed, Edna walked in carrying a huge tray of sliced prime beef along with an assortment of vegetables all garnished with greens on a lovely sterling silver tray. She tried to be very deliberate and cautious as she served the first two guests properly but in attempting to get closer to the third, the tray slipped from her unsteady hands and fell to the ground with a resounding squishy, slurping, thump as deadly silence reigned around the table.

Watching one's guests react with horror as they began cleaning themselves with their napkins, many women, and men for that matter, would possibly lose their cool at this moment but not mother. As we scurried about to clean up the mess, Edna broke out into tears of shame and embarrassment. Mother calmly arose, walked over to her, took her by the hand and consoled her saying, "now now Edna dear, it's only a little slip. Let's go into the kitchen and we'll have steaks ready for everyone in no time."

That did it. Everyone relaxed, we cleaned up the mess, left the table for thirty minutes and came back to some very delicious steaks. Of course mother did the serving as by this time

Edna was laying prostrate on her bed with a cold towel on her forehead.

Just the other day I heard a report on TV that there is now proof positive that a moderate amount of alcohol each day increases a person's HDL ratio and thus decreases heart attacks. Bea must have known about this 50 years ago because she loved to have her daily nip. Many times while she talked to friends on the phone I found her sipping her bourbon, all the while keeping up a string of lively chatter. Other times she had her daily quota when friends came to the house for a few hours of shmoosing (gossiping).

One of her rituals was performed on Thursdays, when grandpa, would come over for lunch. Afterwards, the two of them would sit in the den of our apartment and knock off a fifth of bourbon between them as they just chatted away. Grandpa, a Russian immigrant, was a very accomplished drinker and always carried in his jacket pocket, a silver half-pint flask loaded with booze. Those nips along with the ten cigars a day, I'm sure, kept him going until his death at 85 in 1943. His memory is always brought back when I see or read about that wonderful comedian George Burns who at the age of 100 still admitted to five or six cigars and three or four martinis a day.

Throughout all the years, I only found my mother under the influence once. I came home from high school late one wintry Thursday afternoon and heard her soft voice moaning from the den. When I entered I found her lying on the couch with a cold wet wash cloth over her forehead all the while wailing and chanting,

"My beautiful children, my beautiful children."

While most of us when sick from booze would be praying to God that we would never drink again if He just made us well, mother was thinking not of herself, but her children.

CHAPTER NINETEEN

During the war, World War II that is, the government enacted rationing of foodstuffs, shoes, gasoline, and tires. Whether there was or was not a real shortage of these things or whether it was done just to make everyone cognizant that a war was on, was something that I have never learned for a fact and the history books don't seem to have addressed it.

All I knew at the age of sixteen was around the first of every month mother received ration books in the mail which contained stamps mostly for meat, sugar, coffee and a few other things. She received one book for herself and one book for each of her children and they were to be presented to the grocer when rationed products were purchased. He in turn was supposed to remove the proper stamps and return the book to the customer.

But mother never went into a grocery store as far as I knew. Each morning she would pick up the phone and call Charlie's grocery store located a few blocks from the house, chat with Charlie for a few minutes and then give him an order to be delivered.

Often I was home when the delivery arrived but I never saw her take out any coupons and hand them over even though much of the contents were rationed items. After this had gone on for some years I finally learned how mother was handling the war. On the first delivery of groceries after she received her monthly ration books, she would give all four of them to the deliveryman and that was the extent of her hardship with food shortages during the war. No matter how much she ordered and no matter how often she needed scarce items like steaks, butter, sugar, coffee and the like, they were always delivered to her door, no questions asked. How Charlie handled his end, I never knew, but that surely had something to do with the infamous "black market" that existed throughout the entire war.

As time went on, the war too went on and I was in the process of taking lots of tests given by the Armed Forces branches like the Army Air Corps, Army ASTP college program, the Navy V-5 and V-12 programs and the Marine Air Corps. For some forgotten reason I needed a birth certificate and I went down to City Hall to get one. I gave them my birth date as January 28, 1926 and they kept coming up empty making me think maybe I was an orphan or something of the sort. I don't know why, but somehow the clerk must have thought about looking on the 27th and sure enough I was presented with a birth certificate dated January 27th not 28th. For seventeen years I had celebrated my birthday on the 28th because mother had told me it was so, and I suddenly learned that I was a day older.

I couldn't wait to get home and point out to mom her big boo boo and when I did, she looked at me rather pensively, thought for a moment and said, "I guess daddy was right when he said it was the 27th but I didn't believe him."

Seems as though she always had trouble remembering birth dates. Sometime after she died I took a good look at her marriage certificate that I found in her vault, and found that she had made herself two years younger, 24 instead of 26, and it was deliberate, no mistake. When she started dating Sidney after daddy died, she found that he was three years younger than she was so she lied to him and made herself five years younger or two years younger than Sid. I'll get into that more later.

When I finally was drafted into the Navy in 1944 my fellow recruits and I couldn't have any visitors for the first 6 weeks, but sure enough, on our first official visiting day at Great Lakes there she was with her arms full of salamis, cheeses, and cookies. I was the envy of everyone and this shtupping (filling up-pushing into) with food continued throughout my next two years in service as I continually received packages wrapped in brown paper, loaded with stamps on the outside and goodies on the inside. I still have a snapshot that one of my shipmates took of me just after our first mail call in over a month when our ship arrived in Guantanamo Bay Cuba. The stack of packages was as high as my six-foot frame. Even my buddies who didn't know Aunt Bea loved her for all the good things she sent.

As I think back over those years in service I'm reminded of the fall of 1944 when I caught scarlet fever at the naval base in Gulfport Mississippi. I was hospitalized for almost eight weeks due to complications of one sort or another that had set in. I must have either written mother or called her to tell her about being in the hospital, I can't really say, but one day a nurse came to my bed and told me that mother was out in the hall and that I could get up to visit with her.

I couldn't believe my ears, but, I put on my robe and slippers and padded out to see her standing there with her big rosy cheeks, her navy suit, big hat, huge purse and broad smile. I gave her a hug and got her kisses in return, all the time wondering how in God's name she did it. I never really found out how but this 53 year old woman managed to get a reservation on a train from Chicago to New Orleans during the war when it was literally impossible to do so. She then had to travel the 50 or so miles to the Gulfport Naval station in Mississippi and talk her way onto an active wartime military base to see her son who was in the naval hospital. But she did it and I'll never forget her visit and what the sight of her sparkling smile meant and did for my spirits.

Many months later I was stationed at Navy Pier in Chicago and had the opportunity to leave the base late every afternoon so long as I returned by midnight. On top of that, on any 16 nights of each month that I chose, I could actually return by seven the following morning, so I was one lucky guy. I was able to see all of my old friends who didn't go into service and above all, the girls. Almost every night was spent with one girl or the other and they were all very impressed with my war stories which were all basically good lies, because I had yet to leave the states.

One summer evening I was all decked out in my Navy whites. I was an Electronic Technicians mate 3rd class, and I spent a lot of time preening my hair (I had lots of it then) along with the rest of myself and uniform for a big date with Margie. I took care of the few pimples I had and I really looked great with my sailor hat worn at just the right jaunty and rakish angle and had just the proper kind of salty creases in it as I wore it just above my eyebrows. When I said good-bye to mother she noticed that I had a dirty spot on the left shoulder of my white middy blouse and she exclaimed,

"I'll get something to take that spot out dear" as she scur-ried into the kitchen and returned with a bottle of Chlorox.

She literally poured the fluid onto my shoulder and rubbed it with a cloth for a full minute finally stating,

"There, the spot's gone."

Sure the spot was gone but did I ever reek from the smell of chlorine on my way over to Margie's. She must have thought I was the laundryman when I arrived at her door.

Some hours later, we were at the Chez Paree, at the time, Chicago's premier and most famous night club. Margie and I never left the dance floor as we jitterbugged away to the rhythms of the Count Basie orchestra.

We had been dancing for the entire set of over 40 minutes when I felt something rip in the left shoulder of my blouse. As I turned my head for a closer look I felt an even larger tear and to my disbelief there I stood in the middle of the dance floor with the entire left sleeve of my blouse hanging down below my elbow. The Chlorox had done a number on the cot-ton blouse and eaten away all the stitching that held the sleeve on. I then knew why mother left all the washing to Edna and the laundress.

CHAPTER TWENTY

Mother was never a very religious person. She used God's name quite a bit, thank God for this and thank God for that, but as far as religious participation in the synagogue she only went to temple on the high holidays of Rosh Hashana and Yom Kippur, the Jewish New Year and Day of Atonement.

She was a member of the Anshe Emet synagogue which played it very smart when it came to getting its members to pay their annual dues. Without your dues payment in advance, you would get no reserved seats for the holidays. If your check wasn't received before the holidays you didn't receive entry tickets and without them the ushers wouldn't let you in. That's one reason why the Jewish people are so good at raising funds. If you want to attend High Holiday services, you give. Very simple.

She had been a member of the Temple for many years and always retained the same seats, third row from the rear and near the right sidewall. Quite often I used to go with her and always wondered why she had such terrible seats. I can still clearly see her dressed for temple in her finery which included a huge hat and gloves that were the "de rigueur" of the day.

She and I would invariably get to Temple late and quietly slip into our seats without much notice from anyone. Without fail, after about 30 minutes of prayers I would look over and find her with her eyes closed in apparent sleep. Once in a while when I would nudge her to wake up she would always come back with,

"I'm just resting my eyes sweetheart."

One day after arriving early for a change, I watched the congregation fill up the auditorium, most of them smiling and waving ostentatiously to friends as they moved down the aisles to the more important front section seats. Feeling somewhat belittled, I said to mother, "You can hardly see or hear anything back here mom, nobody even knows we're here."

"Of course darling", she replied, "that's why I keep these seats. Neither the Rabbi nor anyone else knows if I'm sleeping or awake, or for that matter whether I was late or made it here at all,"

CHAPTER TWENTY-ONE

Even though Sidney didn't produce much income for the two of them throughout the years, he loved to play poker at least once or twice a week either at his Moose lodge on Saturday afternoons at the old Morrison Hotel on Madison Street. I have no idea whether or not these were honest games amongst friends or run by the syndicate, but Sid never ever seemed to win. At least that's what he told mother all the time and in return mother would give him what he lost and then some. So it went, every week, year in and year out. Mother and I talked talk about it periodically as she always bemoaned the fact that he was losing all that money. I can't remember how many times I told her to stop taking care of Sid's losses in the poker games or if the words had any effect on her. But one day during lunch she finally vowed,

"No more, I'm going to tell him to quit playing. I won't give him another nickel to lose at his poker game. He never wins." I heartily agreed with her thinking I had won the battle. Then she looked up to me with her typical expression of indecision, and with a pleading look quietly said,

"But what if he should win?"

I knew then, that she would continue to give him the money.

Parties, nobody loved parties more than Aunt Bea. If you gave a party and invited her, she'd be there with bells on. She and Sid would arrive early, leave late and she would love every minute of the time. Every party she ever went to was marvelous, wonderful, beautiful and fun. She never carped or groused about any of them. The people were always dressed beautifully, they danced divinely and everyone was very funny or very sweet.

At a surprise party given in honor of my forty -third birthday she was talking with my dear old friend Harold the optometrist asking him a thousand questions about his work, family, and parents. Quite unexpectedly she said to Harold,

"How old are you dear?"

"51 Aunt Bea," he answered.

With that, mother patted her cheek with her hand and with a startled look on her face said,

"Just the age my Barney was when he dropped dead".

With that, Harold burst into gales of laughter grabbed her and kissed her on her wonderful cheeks.

For a number of years my sister Joyce and brother-in-law Bill lived on Lake Shore Drive just three blocks from mother which of course made mother extremely delighted to have her daughter so near. She spent quite a few afternoons and evenings with the two of them and had the most wonderful time when she and Bill could play gin rummy together. Above all, Bill was the best son-in-law a woman could want, and he always catered to mother's whimsical ideas as though she was his own mother.

Mom, being the night person she was, often would pick up the phone at 9 or 10 o'clock at night and call Joyce and Bill to just talk as all mothers do. At the end of the conversation many times she would get Bill on the line and ask him,

"Whatcha doing now Bill?"

To which he would almost always answer,

"Nothing mom."

Mother would come back with,

"How about some gin rummy?" to which Bill would invariably answer with "why not" and invite her to come over and she would. In those days a four-block walk along Lake Shore Drive posed no peril to anyone much even to a lone woman.

Once there, she and Bill always had a good time together. My sister would go to sleep soon after mother arrived leaving the two of them at the card table. Mother never left much before midnight, and even though Bill got up at five AM he never rushed her out. This went on sometimes once or twice a week for many months and you can bet that Bill would have liked to have called it off but he never did.

That is, until one night after a particularly tough day at the office and a miserable ride through Chicago's rush hour traffic. When mother called at ten winding up with the usual, "Whatcha doing Bill?" he quickly and unexpectedly retorted,

"Ma, I'm fucking your daughter."

Mother just as quickly and smoothly replied,

"That's nice Bill, have a good time. How long should I wait before coming over?"

Mother lived the last 45 years of her life only a few blocks from Wrigley Field the home of the Cubs and Bears. I had season tickets for the Bear games with a couple pals of mine, Kenny, Milt and Ted and so I was able to kill two birds with one stone by visiting mother for lunch before the games.

One day I would bring Ken and another day Milt or Ted. Sometimes we'd all descend upon her, and sometimes we'd even bring along our sons. It never mattered how many people walked into her apartment at 11:30 on the Sunday morning of a Bear game, she always had enough food to choke a horse.

It's almost impossible to describe the onslaught of food that poured out of her kitchen but I'll try.

Shortly after we arrived we would gather around her large dining room table that had orange juice in front of each setting and for good luck, pitchers of grapefruit and pineapple juice. A tray filled with an assortment of warm, toasted and sliced bagels was immediately attacked with gobs of cream cheese, either plain or with chives. A large tray heavily laden with both belly lox and nova, sliced onions and tomatoes alongside kosher pickles got us going in earnest.

While we were slathering the cream cheese and piling up the ingredients of the lox sandwich upon the toasted half bagel, mother would appear with another tray loaded with scrambled eggs and countless pieces of crispy fried hickory smoked bacon. Remember that these were the happy days before the world knew about cholesterol and everyone enjoyed their breakfast meal without hearing someone chastising him about his HDL ratio or his high cholesterol or triglyceride counts.

The purring and yumming that went on at the table with everyone chewing away must have been a great sound to mother for it only encouraged her to bring out some more. In no particular order we were shtupped with fried chicken livers, left over chicken legs and wings, a few smoked fish, halava, American cheese and sliced salami, coffee, milk, apple strudel and a few pieces of chocolate to finish things off. It was the kind of meal that killed more Jews than Hitler.

The guys and I loved every moment of it as we chomped away and got mother to repeat familiar stories that she had told us time and time again over the years, but never remembered telling us. When we were completely sated, and I include the teen-age boys in that statement if it is possible, we would push away from the table claiming Aunt Bea to be the greatest. But she would just look at us pathetically and say,

"You didn't eat a thing. You eat like a bunch of birds," and everyone would moan and groan as they did every week when they heard the same line.

When it came time to leave for the 1 PM kickoff everyone would give her a kiss in the apartment and start down her long hallway toward the elevator. But true to form she would follow the pack, all the while telling us to come back and next time bring our appetites. When the elevator door opened, just as she did when we were kids, she had to give everyone that last kiss and continue to wave good-bye until the elevator door closed and took us to the lobby.

CHAPTER TWENTY-TWO

Some months after mother died I was going through her private papers and I found two very small diaries that she kept between the years 1937 and 1945 into which she made periodic entries. She was 47 and had been going steady with Sid for three years when she began making the entries in them in which she expressed her feelings about his conduct. The following are excerpts from those diaries, feelings that she never outwardly expressed but which must have irritated her sweet soul.

June 13, 1937- Started for a long ride. He (Sidney) told me to put gas in the car. (It was her car as he never owned one.) Was inwardly put out about it because he never said anything about paying me back. Felt bad.

June 20, 1937-He said we would take a streetcar or a bus to the Uptown Theater. Wouldn't take a cab, the cheapskate.

July 4, 1937- I said I like hamburgers and hot dogs. Oh well, 14th Street he said. Was I surprised? (The term 14th street was a slur inferring she was from a low class neighborhood.)

August 1, 1937- I entertained Ben and his wife. Joyce hadn't come home yet at 3AM from South Haven. I was using the carpet sweeper. He sat in the chair and I asked him if he would let his mother use the carpet sweeper. He said, you are not my mother. I said I am a woman, I am a lady.

August 15, 1937-He gave me $2.50 for three tickets I had bought at $.75 each for the show at the Blackstone Hotel. Before he gave me the $2.50 he asked me if I had a quarter change. The cheapskate.

November 6, 1939- After going steady for five years, we went up to visit Helen and while conversing in two different conversations he referred to me as SHE.

Mother seemed to be deeply hurt by some of these seemingly trivial insensitivities of Sid. She was too good and too sweet to have a blowup because of them but one can easily see the hurt pouring into the diary.

We pick up again late in 1941 and carry through to 1945 with the following passages.

August 18, 1941- Went to see Sonja Henie. Instead of sitting in our seats, I sat in some vacant seats on the aisle. He was raving. He said everyone was looking at me because I took someone else's seats. Said it was a lot of guts. Terrible big quarrel. You big shit he said to me.

September 19, 1939- On the trip to New York, Tommy (her nephew) didn't want to dance with Blossom. I told Sid about it. He said, what do you want me to do, hit him?

November 12, 1939- Grandpa did not pay me the money he promised for Tommy's trip to New York. He said, you asked once. You don't have to ask again. Some lawyer.

March 30, 1942- When I called his attention to the funny colored paint on our building's hallways he said, "They want it and that's the way it's going to be." He also said, "there's a war on."

July 9,1942- Going out for the first time to the Villa Venice (an elegant suburban night club) I gave him the money to pay. He was so angry he said, "I don't care if the Villa Venice burns up. Do we have to go just because the Jones's go there?" Afterwards coming home with the Gordon's, not one word. I paid for the evening and the ride on the gondola. He did not even ask me if I wanted a sandwich. I sure was burned up.

August 15, 1942- Upon leaving the house he said to call an electrician because Edna's toilet was stuffed up, instead of saying janitor. Dumb, dumb, dumb.

September 8, 1942-Coming home from the races I was a little upset. He said to me, "What is the matter, is the $100 you gave me bothering you?" Imagine, after all the money I've given him.

December 26, 1942- As he was coming over I asked him to bring me 5 nickels for the phone. He brought exactly five. He could not even think of bringing me five extra ones. Nobody home in his head. Dumb.

December 28, 1942- I gave Edna $3 to give to Mr.Neiman. She met him in the lobby gave him the money and thanked him for the hose he gave her for Christmas. I reminded him that I bought the hose he gave her. He did not even say thanks or even attempt to pay me back.

January 26, 1943- 10 days after his insurance policy expired I had a big quarrel with him. He said he had to go to the doctor and then he would know if he wanted to pay. He is so foolish. No brains. I can not make him understand anything. Very dumb.

January 28, 1943- I gave him $115 today. I left it for Edna to give to him. He asked me to buy a gift for Jerry because he did not have the time. He did not even mention it again after that. Very ignorant-selfish-most contemptible RAT.

January 29, 1943- Berenice and her husband are going to Mexico. We discussed it on our way home. He said Berenice ought to marry Sam and have a child to forget. I told him she needed a husband more than a child. He is so dumb in his opinions.

May 29, 1943- We played gin at Jeannette's. I loaned him $10. He paid me back $8 because I owed him $2 for Jerry's birth certificates. Before I gave him the $10 I loaned him $.50. While giving me back my money he handed me a dollar and took back a fifty-cent piece. Piker. Would not even give me $.50.

February 13, 1944- Played poker at Etta's. First, when I stayed in he said, "sucker." I said let's play deuces wild and he said no. I gave him angry looks.

They had now been going together for 12 years and even though she never gave a hint of it, he must have really been aggravating her but she wouldn't let him go and continued to subsidize his existence. Whether Sid was making much money then I don't think mother ever knew. She was the provider for most things and must have been content with her position.

February 20, 1944- We were over to Eleanor's on Sunday evening and discussed how little he talks. He got angry and said to me "dry up." He said that Jerry should not wear tight pajamas because tight pajamas make a boy passionate. That's why he said dry up because I did not agree with him. (I don't know if he was scientifically right or wrong in that statement but I can tell you that at the age of 18 I most certainly was the horniest man alive, so I guess he wasn't altogether too far off base.)

May 1, 1944- Called me up and said that Saturday night was Eleanor and Fred's anniversary. He said I should get the tickets for the show. I said why don't you and he said he didn't have time. I said I couldn't sit beyond row 5. He said I would sit in the balcony if he wanted me too. He is a big fool. He said he wasted 10 years. I did not waste anything. He sure is a great big fool.

December 18, 1945- We went up to Joe's to play gin. Going down the elevator to go home there was only one Tribune paper left. He took it. He did not insist I have it and that he could get another one. Instead I took the Sun. He let me. He went home with the Tribune. He could have said "You like the Tribune, take it, I can get one on my way home after I leave you." The next day when he called, I told him I did not get my Tribune. He said I insisted on taking the Sun. I told him you did not even tell me you would buy another Tribune on your way home. He said he didn't care. He is very miserable.

December 22, 1945-I told him how thin Eleanor got and he said it is all in the eating. How dumb, dumb, dumb.

December 27, 1945- I had Joyce and Bill over and I was washing the dishes afterwards because I had no maid. I said I wonder where all these dishes came from and he said, "How do I know." Dumb, dumb, dumb

And so it went, each of them needing the other and her resentments seemed to build up by the day.

Chapter Twenty-Three

Finally, when they decided to get married I was in the 6th year of mine and was raising three boys in Highland Park. For all the years during the fifties, sixties and into the seventies, mother and Sid would take the Northwestern train each Sunday and come out to our house in the afternoon. We would sit around the pool in summer and in the den in winter, have chop suey or fried chicken for dinner and watch some TV through the ten o'clock news. then I would drive them to the railroad station to catch the last train back to the city. From shortly after dinner, through the news, Sid would soundly sleep in a big chair while mother would cluck around the children or tell us all how beautiful our house was.

Mother had one particular present that she brought every Sunday, a bag with three or four huge oversized Hershey bars and a smaller bag full of cheese. The chocolate was for the children and the cheese was for our dogs. She just loved feeding them and they were always very excited when she walked through the door bag in hand.

No one loved people or life more than Bea did. I was in the taxi business and gave mother a constant supply of cab coupons that she could use in lieu of cash for cab rides. I assumed that when she went downtown each day she would

enjoy the luxury of a cab instead of standing on corners waiting for the bus in all kinds of weather and fighting for a seat
on a crowded bus.

But one day I was quite surprised when my young cousin
Margie told me how often she saw mother on the bus. In fact
she said, she always looked forward to finding Aunt Bea when
she boarded because she was such a lot of fun and the two of
them would talk all the way to the loop. That was some com-
pliment. One that very few people in their seventies and
eighties could ever hope to get from a lady in her twenties.

Notwithstanding that, what irritated me about the conversation with Margie was the fact that mother was still riding
the bus while I was continuing to send her coupons to take a
cab. Where were the coupons going?

The next time we were together I confronted her with my
evidence that I recently obtained from her niece and she con-
fessed. She gave all of the coupons to Sidney so that he could
take a cab instead of a bus because he was finding it difficult
to walk. (He never had trouble getting to a dinner table). As
for her, she admitted she really preferred the bus because
there was no one to talk with in a cab, while on the bus, she
always found a conversational companion. It was just no fun
for mother to ride alone in a cab.

Going to a funeral home to pay respects to friends and relatives always seemed to be a highlight of the week for Bea. Of
course, in her later years, funerals became more and more
common. When she heard about a death, usually over the
phone, she would proceed to talk about the person for the

next fifteen minutes relating stories and always saying what a wonderful person the deceased was.

But the visitation at the Chapel was the "piece de resistance." At the proper hour she would get all dressed up including her big hat, grab Sidney and take off for the funeral parlor which to her meant a gathering, an affair, a party. She would cluck around the bereaved, make her sweet words and remain until the place closed, all the while talking with whomever happened to be around, whether they be friend or unknown.

When my father-in-law died in 1970 we were at Piser's Funeral Chapel on Broadway in Chicago gathered in mourning when mother entered. I was up and around talking with most everyone, friends, business acquaintances and employees. When I spied her I gave her a big hug and after she embraced my wife she took off to look at the deceased in the open casket. While she was standing in front of the coffin, Milt, one of my dearest friends, went up to her and gave a great big kiss to his Aunt Bea. As soon as he let her go she exclaimed,

"Milty, doesn't Morris look good. I never saw him look so well."

This caused Milt to break into a huge smile but when she followed it up with,

"And isn't Jerry a wonderful host the way he talks to everybody," he broke out into a gale of laughter within the confines of that most somber chapel.

CHAPTER TWENTY-FOUR

We had all gathered in my sister Joyce's apartment on Lake Shore Drive to celebrate mother's 80th birthday. All we heard prior to and during the evening was mother whispering to each of us, "Don't tell Mr. Neiman how old I am."

Just my sisters, our spouses, a couple of friends and a few grandchildren were present. Of course everyone brought a gaily-wrapped present for this beautiful lady. After dinner, mother became comfortably ensconced on the sofa with all her presents around her. She began opening them one by one, first, reading the card aloud and then commenting on how sweet the words were. When the gift was opened you would have thought it was from Gucci's or Tiffany's from the time she spent raving about it.

One present was held back till the very end. It was from Bill, a fine artist and architect in his own right, and we all knew what was inside the wrapping. The gift itself was in a box that was about 3 inches high, four inches wide and a foot long. When mother slowly unwrapped the birthday paper one could hear snickers in the group along with hushed whispers as the box was laid bare.

Mother made all sorts of wild guesses about what could be in the box, and how beautiful the box was. She slowly proceeded to lift the hinged top to reveal a perfectly sculpted clay replica of a man's penis that was even larger than life size and perfect in every respect. Bill and mother always had a good relationship and he could kid her about anything and she loved every word. Above all, Bill was the best son-in-law a woman could want, and he always catered to mother's whimsical ideas.

When the penis was exposed we all bit our lips to keep from laughing. We oohed and aahed as we waited expectantly for the words about how beautiful it was. But instead, mother gently put the box down on the coffee table and asked where her purse was, a question she asked at least once or twice every night that we were together.

Her grandson Barney gave her purse to her which she opened, removed her compact and set it down on the coffee table. She slowly opened the compact, took a quick peek at herself in the mirror and removed the powder puff from within. With great deliberation she then patted every inch of the penis applying powder to its entirety and when she stopped she looked up and exclaimed,

"There, now it looks like a real shmuck."

CHAPTER TWENTY-FIVE

Some months later in that same year, 1970, when she was eighty, mother informed us that her doctor had found a small lump on her left breast and advised her to have a biopsy performed immediately. Joyce and I both lived in the city at that time and we asked the usual questions of the doctor and discussed every choice and procedure with both he and mother.

Mother decided on the operation and we all agreed with her knowing full well that she would do whatever she wanted to do anyway. The one ominous warning that the doctor gave her was that if the biopsy proved malignant, he would vigorously advise a mastectomy. That became pretty frightening for me and I'm sure to mother also, but she never showed any reluctance for the operation or any fear of her impending misfortune.

I drove mother to the hospital on the appointed day so that she could undergo all the pre op necessities that were required. The following morning I walked beside her gurney until it disappeared behind the swinging doors of the operating room that were emblazoned NO ADMITTANCE in huge red letters. We had nothing more to do but to bite our nails and wait in a state of anxiety.

After an hour or so the doctor appeared with that serious look upon his face that told us without a word being uttered that he would have to perform the mastectomy which we all had feared.

Once our fears were confirmed, a pall of sadness fell over us like a heavy gray overcast as we thought about our 80-year mother and questioned how she would tolerate the operation and how she would react emotionally to such radical surgery. But knowing our mother as we did, we were sure there was no way in the world that this event would change her life one iota and it didn't.

Some hours later, her spunk and bright spirit burst from behind those dark clouds within a few minutes after leaving the recovery room. As she was being wheeled to her private room at the Northwestern Hospital. I fell in step with the attendant and walked alongside of her, again holding her wonderfully soft hand and asked, "How do you feel sweet-heart?" Without a moment's hesitation she raised her eyes to meet mine and shot back,

"Hitler should feel like I feel."

I immediately knew that mother hadn't changed a bit and never would. Sure she lost a part of her body but her soul and spirit remained deeply constant. Those were the only unkind words I ever heard her utter about anyone dead or alive, and God knows that wishing Hitler's soul the worst was not even close to a defamation of any sort.

When the cart was wheeled into her room, my sister followed it in and the nurses of course asked me to stay outside until they got mother set up and comfortable in her bed. After about fifteen minutes of pacing in the halls I was able to enter along with Sidney who had been waiting outside with me. I stepped back and let Sidney approach her first. He gave her a gentle kiss on her cheek and gently asked, "How are you dearie?"

They conversed briefly but I couldn't make out a word of what mother was saying. When it was my turn, I noticed that she had been keeping her hand close to her mouth all the while she talked with Sid and so I asked her if something was wrong with her lips.

"No sweetheart," she whispered, "I don't have my teeth in and I don't want Mr. Neiman to see me without them." Eighty years old and the feminine vanity was still with her and would never leave as long as she lived.

Five days later, early in the afternoon of a cold and dreary Thursday, I drove to the hospital as mother was being discharged and needed a ride home. After parking the car I rode the elevator up to her 14th floor room and found her almost fully dressed as she and my sister Joyce were collecting her things in anticipation of her imminent discharge.

When I felt that everyone was ready I grabbed her bag and started for the door saying I would bring the car around. I paused momentarily when she asked me to wait a moment. As I turned around I found her pulling sheet after sheet of Kleenex from the box beside her bed and was rolling them into a ball. Without hesitation she then stuffed the entire wad into the brassiere cup which once held her missing breast. She made a few tugs on her dress, pulled things around, pushed others, stood up straight in front of the full length mirror and finally said to no one in particular, "There, now that looks real." Let's go."

I could only look first at my sister, then at mother and give her a big hug saying, "You look sexier than ever mom."

CHAPTER TWENTY-SIX

My niece Mallory and her husband had the family over one gloomy winter Sunday in 1975. It was a typical family gathering with her two daughters running around the place, her father, Bill, telling funny stories, Sidney sleeping in the huge lounge chair, and mother looking for her purse.

After devouring a Chinese take out dinner, the evening continued with Mallory showing the usual home movies of her and the children. Mother clucked her tongue incessantly about her great grandchildren and raved about how beautiful they looked and smart they were.

There was really nothing out of the ordinary in the films until Mallory slipped a porno flick into the projector without any announcement of what was to come. We all caught on quickly because one doesn't commonly see naked women and men cavorting about in home movies, especially those of your relatives. All except mother, that is, who continued to closely watch the action all the time saying that her granddaughter Mallory was so beautiful and had such a nice figure as she referred to the naked blonde romping all over the screen. We all got a great kick of those comments, but we said nothing expecting more comments and more giggles. By this time even Sidney had awakened from his deep dream of peace and intently devoured the scenes flashing on the screen before his eyes. He hadn't said a word for the past hour but couldn't resist commenting when he saw the naked girls,

"Boy what she could do for my sex life," he proclaimed, to which mother quickly retorted in Yiddish, "gornish helfin." (nothing would help.) Not a bad comeback for an 83 year old woman.

CHAPTER TWENTY-SEVEN

Mother loved to eat. She had a wonderful appetite and never gained any weight because of it. Taking her out to a restaurant was always a treat for us because she relished every moment of the meal. Don't get me wrong. Going out for dinner to a restaurant was not a novelty for her by any means. What was great was how she savored each and every meal in each and every restaurant.

After comfortably seating herself, she was always ready for a little bourbon to sharpen her taste buds. Then she would listen attentively as the waitperson intoned the liturgy of the specials. While the rest of us would scan the menus and ask the usual "what are you having", of each other, mother, without a word to anyone would gently push herself from the table and slowly amble away. We all knew where she was going and it wasn't to the ladies room.

She had a much more important purpose for the hike. She wanted to see what everyone else in the restaurant was eating and would slowly and purposefully walk around the floor periodically stopping to chat with a diner here and a diner there. I always watched her with a bit of dumb embarrassment, as I was sure that sooner or later someone would react angrily to her interruption. To the contrary, she always brought a smile to the person that she disturbed. In her own way she was checking out the menu by asking different diners what they were eating and how it tasted.

Upon her return to the table she was always ready when the waitperson returned for orders and was quick to make her selection known. When everyone was finally served his or her entrees, we were all always able to recite in unison with her as soon as she began to speak,

"Did you ever see so much food in your life?" as she clucked her tongue in amazement at the amount of food on the plate and then proceeded to devour everything on it.

Mother was always a party person and loved to make every gala affair that she could. She'd be the first to arrive and the last to leave. My surprise 50th birthday party which Marlene threw for me a few months before we were married, was no exception.

Marlene had known my mother for a few years prior to the party, as she and her ex husband were social friends of ours. But for the life of her, mother had a terrible time remembering Marlene's name and always referred to her as "the pretty one." And true to fashion, Marlene adored mother.

When I walked into the house to the roar of "surprise" from about 50 guests, the first face that I saw was mother's as she sat beaming with pride at her "sonny boy." It was a festive gathering and as the evening wore on, guests began to depart around twelve. But mother neither grew weary, tired, or even yawned.

She was 85 at the time and seemed to thrive on the gaiety of the evening. By three AM there were only two couples left, mother and Sid and Pete and Helen, the couple that drove them.

Mother was sipping a bourbon, Sid was asleep and the others, forty years her junior, were ready to pass out from exhaustion when I gave her a hug and a kiss and told her to go home already. Asking where her purse was, she got up with great reluctance and they left amid a flurry of goodbye kisses.

CHAPTER TWENTY-EIGHT

That winter, mother and Sid flew down to Miami Beach for three months, a trip they made each year to get away from Chicago's miserable snow and cold. They always stayed at the Singapore Hotel in Bal Harbor and were well known to everyone on the staff, from the lady who ran the news and sundries shop to the waitresses who whipped up her grilled American cheese sandwiches each day, and from the hotel manager who walked the floor daily and stopped to chat with her down to the bell men whom she greeted every day with a smile.

I had to make a business trip down there during February and called her to tell her when I would be over to visit her at the hotel. She of course was excited to know that I was coming. I could feel it in her voice that she was eager to know I would soon be there, and we would have lunch together.

I arrived right on the stroke of twelve and upon entering the lobby of the hotel I spied mother sitting facing me while seated in an oversized lounge chair directly across from the doorway. We greeted each other with many kisses, they never stopped during her entire lifetime, chatted awhile and then I suggested lunch. She arose and we walked arm in arm over to the hotel restaurant where we had a delightful lunch and talked about the family, Sidney and what was happening in Chicago.

When the check arrived, I paid it and waited while she took a few minutes to say good-bye to the waitress. She asked where her purse was. We found it and slowly ambled back to the lobby to continue our visit. I looked about for a place to sit that would be bright and comfortable but she seemed to be pressing me on back toward the area in which she was sitting when I first arrived. Sure enough she was aiming for the same chair she had occupied earlier, only this time a nicely dressed businessman was sitting in it reading the Miami Herald and enjoying his pipe.

I kind of pulled mother to the side because there were other chairs in the area, but no, she kept going until she stopped beside the man with the pipe and just looked down upon him without saying a word. Within a few moments, obviously sensing mother's nearness, he looked up into her thoughtful face.

"Sonny," she said, "you're sitting in my chair." With that, he sprung up from the chair, half bowed and with a sweeping motion of his arm exclaimed,

"I'm so sorry, please sit down," as she gracefully took the seat with an appreciative,

"Thank you sir. You are a nice man."

CHAPTER TWENTY-NINE

Both Sid and mother were two of the healthiest persons I've ever known. Aside from childbirth and the mastectomy, mother never spent a day in the hospital in her lifetime. Neither of them ever seemed to get sick until 1978 when Sid was hospitalized at Northwestern Hospital for some kind of respiratory ailment. Marlene and I were both concerned about leaving mother alone in her apartment so we asked her to stay with us for a couple of nights until Sid was released.

She reluctantly agreed and one night after returning from the hospital where we all visited Sid, mother, Marlene and I sat in the dining room and had some ice cream before getting ready for bed.

When that time came, Marlene went with mother to the guest bedroom to help her prepare for bed while I cleaned up. Marlene took the bedspread off, made sure mother had enough blankets and showed her where everything was in both the bedroom and the bath. Finally when mother was in bed, we both kissed her goodnight and Marlene and I retired to our room immediately adjacent to mother's. After some time passed, Marlene got into bed with me and before long the two of us began making love in the dark confines of our bedroom. After a few minutes of this delightful pastime, Marlene whispered in my ear,

"I think mother is in the room with us."

Slightly shocked, I softly said, "You've got to be kidding."

"I'm not", she confirmed, and I spoke out asking "Mother, is that you."

From the darkness she replied, "Yes darling. Marlene dear, I can't find my purse."

Quickly, we both scurried about amongst the sheets and in the dark I grabbed my robe and led mother back to her room to look for the missing purse while Marlene quickly threw on her dressing gown. Within moments Marlene held up the misplaced purse much to mother's relief.

Mother returned to bed and Marlene and I quickly resumed our activity which had been disrupted only to have Marlene once again whisper, "Jer, I think she's back."

This time, when I challenged into the darkness of the room, I was answered with, "Darlings, I can't find my earrings." needless to say, our attempts at love making melted away.

The next morning I awoke to find our bedroom brightly awash in sunlight. I put on my robe and opened the bedroom door intent on seeing how mother was doing. The door opened into an L shaped hallway that contained four other doors, one to the reception hall, one to the den, one to a bathroom and one to mother's bedroom. When I entered the hall I found mother standing there in her robe looking a little perplexed as she said to me.

"I've been trying to find my way out of here for five minutes, how do I get out?"

Sound strange from an alert 86 year old woman? It really shouldn't. Every door in the hall was closed and each had been wallpapered with the same fabric that was on the walls thus making the entire area look like solid walls without doors. Poor mom, she was a little confused by all that.

CHAPTER THIRTY

As the year 1978 rolled by, we helped mother celebrate her 89th birthday on May 3 but now she was getting to the point where she needed even more help than Sidney could give her so we brought in Lena to help her through the day. Lena was fabulous. She had worked many years for my sister Joyce and knew mother well and took good care of her.

But even with Lena's help it wasn't enough as she couldn't stay at night and mother was beginning to frequently fall on her way to the bathroom from her darkened bedroom. The specter of a nursing home arose and it was no fun talking about what we were going to have to do for mother. Sid wasn't much help himself at that time, so Joyce and I had to make the decision.

Mother kept slipping and periodically failed to recognize us, all the while talking about things that happened to her when she was a young girl or just married for the first time.

After checking about, I found the Wellington Nursing Home just three blocks from our apartment and made arrangements for mother to take up residence there. We told her about her move but she didn't understand too much of what we said and Marlene and I were chosen to put her in the car for the short trip to the home and have her registered.

It was a bright, clean, well managed and attended home and she was admitted into a two-bed room which was occupied by another elderly lady. By a pure trick of fate the other lady turned out to be my best friend Kenny's mother, Julia, who was in the same condition as my mother. The next three months of watching mother deteriorate are blanked out in my mind. I can barely remember seeing her sit in a wheel chair at the dinner table with a terrible vacant stare in her eyes. This woman who for a lifetime only carried a smile and brought kindness to everyone was reduced to lifelessness. I don't want to think about those scenes or even try to remember what went on. To watch a beloved person lose their God given dignity is most unbearable and best forgotten.

Marlene and I had an apartment in Acapulco Mexico that we vacationed at for a few weeks every January and then again in early spring. This January's intended visit became a little different because of mother's weakening condition. We talked with her doctor to get his advice on whether we should go or not. "By all means go," he said explaining that mother could live on for a long time.

Thus, we bade our good-byes to mother even though we weren't sure she understood and took off for Acapulco. Joyce and Bill met us down there and a good time was had by all. Even though we all knew mother was going to die soon, the stories about her that we repeated to each other for those two weeks, kept us smiling.

When it was time for our return flight to Chicago, a violent 15 inch snowstorm hit the city closing O'Hare Field and we were unable to return on the fifteenth as planned. Influential friends at American Airlines in Acapulco were able to get us out the next day but Joyce and Bill were forced to stay even longer.

Arriving back in the city all we could see were mounds of snow as the cab made its way down the Kennedy Expressway on its way to our condo building on Lake Shore Drive. Little did we know that this snowstorm was to be the downfall of the then Mayor Bilandic who would be defeated in the Democratic primary two weeks later by the now infamous Jane Byrne who became mayor and effected my life greatly over the next few years.

Throwing our luggage into the apartment, we quickly walked the three blocks to the Wellington Manor to see how mother was doing. The nurse in attendance told us that mother had been asking for me quite often and was sure she would be ecstatic to see me. Entering the room we found mother abed with her eyes closed in a light sleep and we went beside her to feel and kiss her still apple like rosy cheeks.

After just a few moments she opened her eyes and broke into a broad but rather weak smile as I said,

"We're home sweetheart."

"I love you darling" is all she uttered as she gently closed her eyes and returned to sleep. I repeated the phrase "I love you" and we downheartedly returned home. Two hours later the phone rang and the nurse told me that mother had died. When I arrived, just a few minutes later, the nurse took me aside and said, "Mr. Feldman, I just wanted you to know that

I am certain that mother was staying alive just to see you once more before dying. It's what kept her alive for this past week."

The city was tied up by the snowfall. The cemetery ground was too hard to open up for the grave and it was difficult for people to even pay respects. Joyce and Bill arrived two days later and memorial services were held before a very small congregation of family and friends who could get to the funeral home.

Five days after she died, they were able to open the ground and we finally found ourselves at graveside at Waldheim cemetery where mother was being buried next to my father. According to her wishes she wanted to be buried in the plot on his left rather than the one on his right because the right side was next to a narrow, wagon rutted roadway and mother told me a hundred times not to put her there because

"It will be too easy for someone to steal me from it."

It was a typical Chicago Mid-January day when mother was lowered into the earth. We were hip deep in snow, the temperature was about 15, the wind screamed but for a change the sky was clear blue. As I walked sadly away from her grave site with Marlene on my arm, I heard the roar of a jet plane high up in the sky and as I looked up I became an awestruck seven year old boy again and mother was once again telling me about the first plane she ever saw.

CHAPTER THIRTY-ONE

It was several months later when Mar and I were cleaning out drawers in mother's old apartment in preparation of renting it out. Sid had moved in with his sister and we never heard from him again. In a drawer we found a second safety vault key for the First National Bank of Chicago and being her executor I made arrangements to open the box.

The day before my appointment at the bank, Marlene and I talked about what we might find in the box. Would it be stuffed with stocks or bonds?. Would there be cash there? Maybe mother kept gold coins or diamonds from the old days in it. Who knew?

Weeks earlier I had opened her main vault box and found little of value. There were about ten various savings account books all stamped closed, at least twenty worthless life insurance policies that the newspapers used to promote for a quarter a week, a half dozen gold coins, and her will. I also found her marriage certificate to my father which brought a smile when I noted I noted that she had lied about her age and made herself two years younger.

I took a cab downtown and upon entering the safety box area, I presented the newly found key to the vault custodian. He inserted his key and after opening the vault door he took out a long black box and handed it to me. Sure enough, I felt weight, there was something in there, but what? With great suspense and excitement I walked over to the nearest available private booth, put the box down and opened the latch to reveal—a stack of canceled checks about six inches thick, maybe four hundred.

Removing the rubber band from around them I first noticed the dates, 1937, 1942, 1947. Looking at the payee's name I discovered that each check was made out to I. Sidney Neiman in various amounts ranging from $25 to $150. She had paid a vault fee for almost 30 years just to save those worthless checks. I don't really know why she kept them all those years. If I ever meet her again, and I pray that I will, I'll be sure to ask.